HAL LEONARD

FOLK HARP METHOD

BY MAEVE GILCHRIST

PLAYBACK+
Speed • Pitch • Balance • Loop

To access audio, visit:
www.halleonard.com/mylibrary

Enter Code
6255-0821-7989-1988

Tracks performed by Maeve Gilchrist
Photography by Jason Jong

ISBN 978-1-4768-1207-6

Visit Hal Leonard Online at **www.halleonard.com**

Explore the entire family of Hal Leonard products and resources

World headquarters, contact:
Hal Leonard
7777 West Bluemound Road
Milwaukee, WI 53213
Email: info@halleonard.com

In Europe, contact:
Hal Leonard Europe Limited
1 Red Place
London, W1K 6PL
Email: info@halleonardeurope.com

In Australia, contact:
Hal Leonard Australia Pty. Ltd.
4 Lentara Court
Cheltenham, Victoria, 3192 Australia
Email: info@halleonard.com.au

CONTENTS

INTRODUCTION

Folk harp is a term generally used for non-classical harps, including the Celtic harp (Irish and Scottish harps) and the lever harp. It is a small- to medium-sized instrument commonly used in folk music settings.

Praise Him with the sound of the trumpet: praise Him with the psaltery and harp.

–Psalm 150:3

The earliest reference to harps in literature is in the psalms of the Hebrew Bible, dating back to 1000 B.C., though earlier instruments such as the Egyptian harp date back to approx 2500 B.C. There is evidence to show that the harp has been used, in one form or another, for thousands of years, in many cultures across the globe – often treasured as a near mythical instrument, shrouded in mystery sometimes bordering on the supernatural.

Rich harping traditions exist today in many areas of the world, including South America, Africa, and Europe. In this book we'll focus on the harp as an instrument of Celtic music. Nowhere was the harp as celebrated as in medieval Ireland, where it experienced a Golden Age between the ninth and 17th centuries. During that period, the schools of Irish harp playing were much revered around Europe and the players held esteemed positions in society. It is still used today as an internationally recognizable symbol of Irish culture.

In both Ireland and Scotland, with their shared Gaelic culture, the original instruments were wholly diatonic, strung with wire and played with the fingernails. This created a haunting, bell-like sound. As musical fashions changed, the single-action pedal harp was introduced in 18th century Europe. Most players switched to gut-string instruments and started playing with the pads of their fingers, as most players still do today.

To extend the harmonic possibilities of the instrument, levers were introduced to Celtic harps, allowing the player to raise each individual string by a half step, playing a similar role to the pedals on the classical harps.

In North America and Europe, the harp is commonly tuned in E♭. Again, this was the influence of the single-action pedal harp, giving the harpist access to three flat keys (E♭, B♭, F), C major, and four sharp keys (G, D, A, E).

There seems to be something truly unique and magical about the sound of the harp that draws in the listener and moves people in an unfathomable way. In this book, we will try to demystify the playing process, bringing in each finger at a time and introducing some general musical concepts in order to provide a solid foundation to you as a beginning harpist.

There is no shortcut around practice. The more you play, the more comfortable and fluid you will become on the instrument. Spend some solid time on hand position and fundamental technique. This will set up your hands and enable you to phrase and control your playing in a musical way. Find other musicians with whom you can play music. Listen. Become inspired and, most importantly, enjoy!

THE FOLK HARP

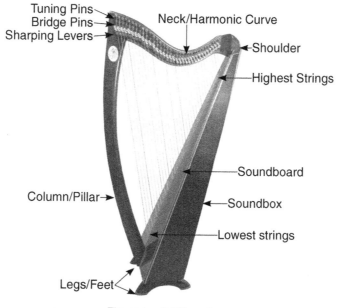

Tuning Pins
Bridge Pins
Sharping Levers
Neck/Harmonic Curve
Shoulder
Highest Strings
Soundboard
Column/Pillar
Soundbox
Lowest strings
Legs/Feet

Thormalen Ceili lever harp

STRINGS

The red strings on your harp are Cs. The black strings are F. The strings are strung in the following order: C, D, E, F, G, A, B, C.

LEVERS

Each string has its own lever. When we raise a lever, it leans onto the string, increasing the tension and raising the pitch of the note by a half step. When we put the lever down, it releases the note to its original tension and pitch.

Using levers enables us to raise and lower our notes, moving through many keys and play non-diatonic (chromatic) harmony.

In some cases, folk harps come without levers. Although it is recommended that you think about adding levers to your harp to expand your options, this book is manageable without. If your harp does not have levers, you should tune it to the key of C major. A number of pieces in this book are in C major and as we move to the keys of G major, D major, and – occasionally – F major, you can simply tune the strings manually. (See the Tuning section that follows for key signature details.)

TUNING

It is best to tune your harp in E♭. This allows a good range of keys on your instrument: four sharp keys (G major, D major, A major, E major), the neutral key of C major, and three flat keys (F major, B♭ major, E♭ major).

Electronic Tuner

It is important to familiarize yourself with your levers right from the beginning of playing the harp. This will help you get the most out of your instrument.

The easiest and most accurate way of tuning your harp is to purchase an electronic tuner calibrated to the standard tuning of A = 440hz.

To tune in the key of E♭, make sure all levers are down and tune your strings in the following order, starting with C and working your way up the octave:

C, D, E♭, F, G, A♭, B♭ (E♭ major, three flats).

Tuning Key

NOTE: Depending on how many octaves you have, continue tuning the harp octave by octave in the same way.

KEY SIGNATURES

A key signature indicates which sharps (#) and flats (♭) are used to determine the tonal center of the selection you are playing. Different pieces of music are played in different keys. Though we will stay in the familiar folk keys (C, G, D) for the majority of this book, as you branch out to play with other musicians, knowing your key signatures and where they lie on your instrument will prove very helpful.

Sharp: A sharp (#) indicates that the pitch of a note is to be raised a half step

Flat: A flat (♭) indicates that the pitch of a note is to be lowered a half step

IF YOUR HARP IS TUNED IN E♭, THESE ARE ALL THE KEYS THAT ARE AVAILABLE TO YOU:

E♭ Major (three flats: B♭, E♭, A♭)
All levers down. Open strings.

F Major (one flat: B♭)
A and E levers up.

B♭ Major (two flats: B♭, E♭)
A levers up.

C Major (neutral: no sharps, no flats)
A, E, and B levers up.

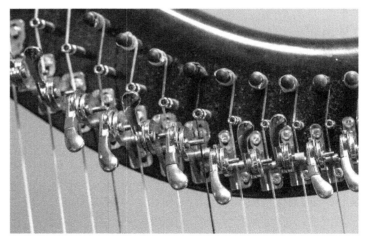

G Major (one sharp: F♯)
A, E, B, and F levers up.

A Major (three sharps: F♯, C♯, G♯)
A, E, B, F, C, and G levers up.

D Major (two sharps: F♯, C♯)
A, E, B, F, and C levers up.

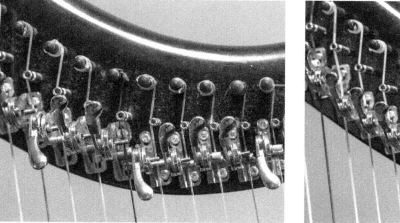

E Major (four sharps: F♯, C♯, G♯, D♯)
A, E, B, F, C, G, and D levers up.\

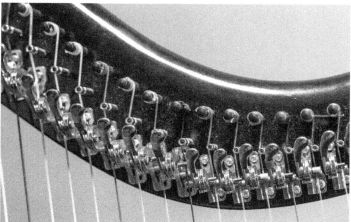

Now put your harp in the key of C major and we are ready to begin.

SITTING WITH THE HARP

When you sit down with your harp, the shoulder of the instrument should be close to the height of your shoulder. You should be sitting comfortably and relaxed with the harp between your legs and resting on your right shoulder. Refrain from leaning around the left side of the harp to see the strings from a closer angle. You'll get used to your sight line from this seated position and it's important to keep a fairly straight spine to maintain a healthy back.

HAND POSITION

Have your right wrist area resting gently on the soundboard as your right hand sits on the strings. The thumb should sit higher than the other fingers, which should be gravitating down slightly.

Your left elbow should float lightly out and up to ensure that your left forearm supports your left wrist. Again, the thumb should sit higher on the strings, with the other fingers pointing slightly downward.

As you pluck the strings, your thumbs should come down over your fingers. Your fingers should curl up creating a complete fist. This fist becomes your rest position and is necessary to keep the hand and wrist relaxed. By moving your fingers into a fist after every note, as much as possible, you also allow the note to ring out, creating the clearest tone.

As you start playing, be patient with yourself and take time to check your hand position frequently, re-adjusting and working your hands. This will benefit your playing at all levels.

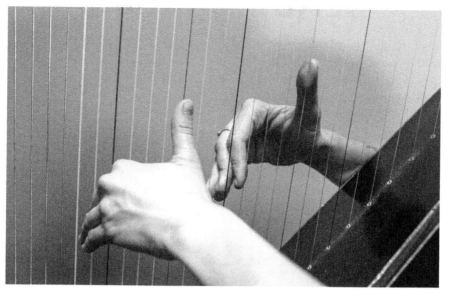

Both hands resting on the harp. Left elbow out and up and right wrist resting on soundboard.
Thumbs up, fingers down.

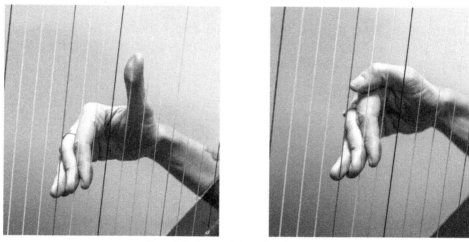

Thumb before and after plucking a string.

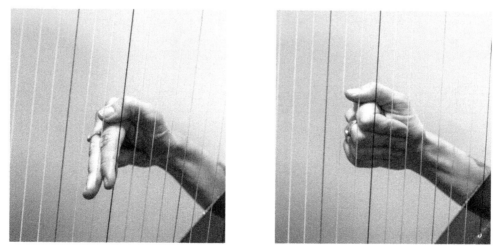

Forefinger and middle finger before and after plucking two strings.

NOTE: Be careful not to contort your hand into what we in the harp world call "the claw." This happens when the student is reaching *up* to the strings, unsupported by the wrist and forearm with all fingers and thumb hitting the strings at the same point on the strings. This is unhealthy for the wrist and makes it impossible to cross fingers over and place the fingers in a way that is conducive to musical phrasing. This is a technique mistake that is most commonly made by the more mature student who lacks flexibility in the wrists and fingers.

READING MUSIC

Music notes are named after the first seven letters of the alphabet: A-B-C-D-E-F-G. By their position on the staff, they can represent the entire range of musical sound.

Clef signs help to organize the staff so notes can be read easily.

TREBLE CLEF AND STAFF

The **treble clef** is used for notes in the higher registers. It has evolved from a stylized letter G and is also known as the G clef. The treble clef's curl circles around the line on which the note G is placed. This is the G above middle C. Notes on the **treble staff** will be played, for the most part, with the right hand.

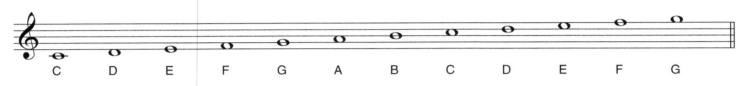

BASS CLEF AND STAFF

The **bass clef** is used for notes in the lower registers. It has evolved from a stylized letter F and is also known as the F clef. The two dots of the bass clef are on each side of the line which the note F is placed. This is the F below middle C. Notes on the **bass staff** will be played, for the most part, with the left hand.

THE GRAND STAFF

The **grand staff** is formed when the treble and bass clefs are connected by a brace and a line. The grand staff is a prominent feature in music for the harp, as well as music for the piano and other keyboard instruments.

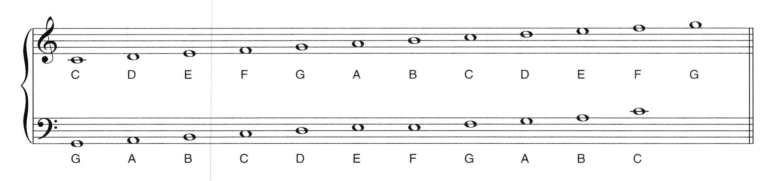

NOTE DURATIONS

4/4 time, also known as common time, has four beats per measure. (For more information on Time Signatures, see page 21.) Within that rhythmic structure, we can assign note values as follows:

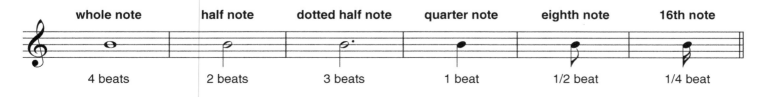

whole note	half note	dotted half note	quarter note	eighth note	16th note
4 beats	2 beats	3 beats	1 beat	1/2 beat	1/4 beat

FINGER PLACING

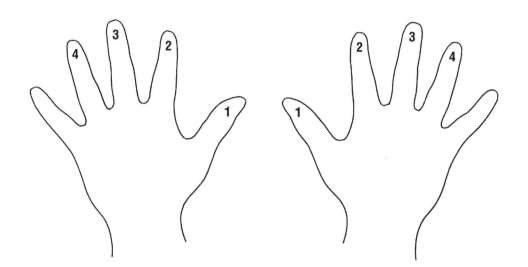

Placing our fingers in an order that will help hand navigation and musical phrasing is an essential tool for any harper. This is called **placing**. Throughout this book you will see finger numbers in brackets. These bracketed numbers represent which fingers should be set on the strings at the same time. Although this seems like a daunting task for the beginner, you will quickly get into the flow of placing your fingers and will internalize the placing techniques so that soon you will not need to read the brackets to know the most effective placing methods.

As a general rule, placing is directional. We are placing as many fingers as we can on the strings as long as they are moving in the same direction, either up or down. The idea is that there are never *no* fingers on the strings unless it's a conscious decision or at the end of a phrase. This phrasing is making sure that your fingers are always one step ahead of what you are playing and will allow you the most *legato* (smoothest) sound.

NOTE: Due to the short length of the little finger, we rarely – if ever – use it for harp playing.

STARTING TO PLAY

We'll start by using our 1st and 2nd fingers in these two finger exercises. Remember, fingers into fist and thumb over fingers!

TWO-FINGER EXERCISES

TRACK 1

TWO-FINGER ETUDE

TRACK 2

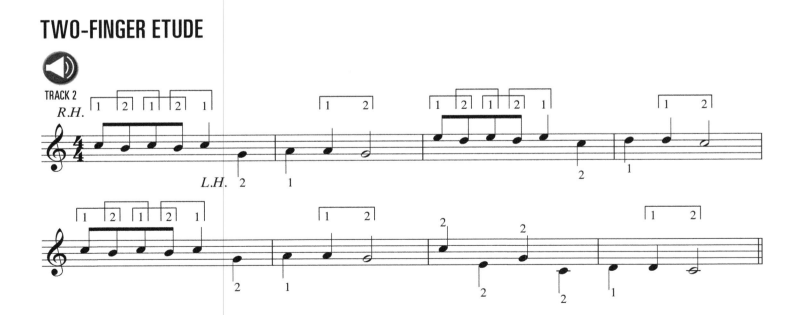

TRIADS

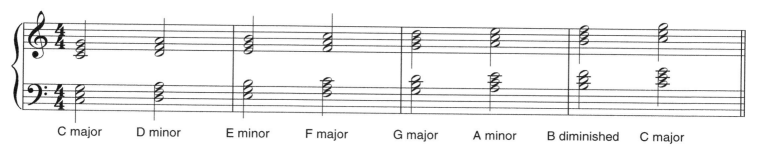

C major D minor E minor F major G major A minor B diminished C major

A **triad** is a three-note chord that is stacked in thirds. These three notes are referred to as (from lowest to highest) the root, the third, and the fifth.

We will now use our 1st, 2nd, and 3rd fingers in these triadic exercises.

C major triad

fifth
third
root

TRIADIC EXERCISES

Triads are a wonderful and essential beginning to understanding harmony and chords. The following exercises are all triads:

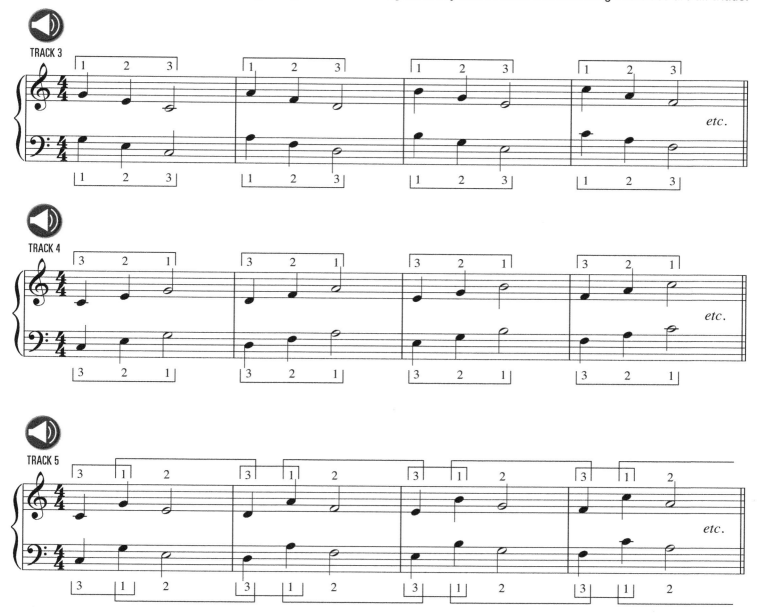

TRACK 3

TRACK 4

TRACK 5

FOUR-FINGER EXERCISES

Now let's bring in the 4th finger in the following exercises. Play all these etudes hands separately and then together.

EXERCISE 1

TRACK 6

EXERCISE 2

TRACK 7

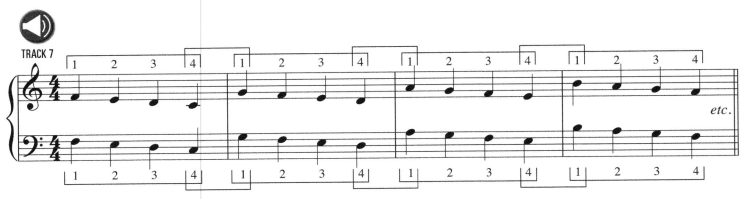

EXERCISE 3

In this ladder-like exercise, you are placing everything one note at a time. Go slowly, resetting your hand, pushing thumb up and fingers down.

TRACK 8

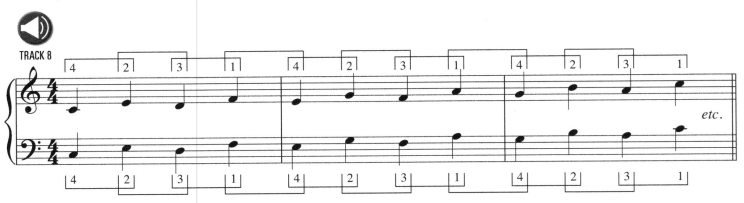

EXERCISE 4

This etude is an octave scale. Ascending: Before playing your thumb, cross your 4th finger under the F and set it on the G string. Descending: Before playing your 4th finger, cross your thumb over and set it on the F.

Now utilize these techniques in the pieces that follow.

FRÈRE JACQUES

TRACK 9

French Folksong

Now try playing it one octave higher!

HYMN

TRACK 10

Traditional Melody

KATIE BAIRDIE

TRACK 11

Scottish Folksong

A MINOR TUNE

BRETON TUNE

Traditional Melody

INTERVALS

An interval is the distance between two notes. Different intervals create different sounds on their own or within a chord.

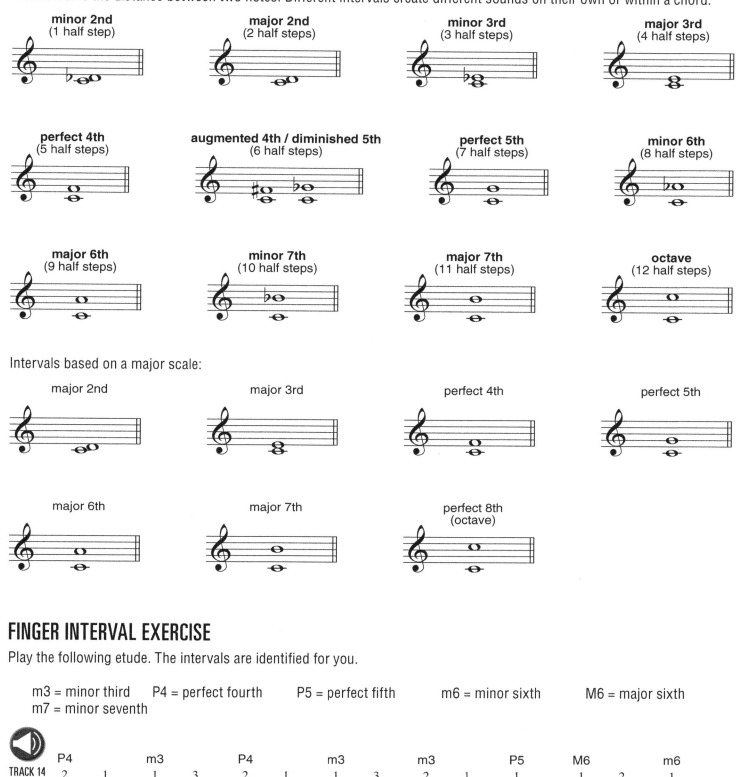

Intervals based on a major scale:

FINGER INTERVAL EXERCISE

Play the following etude. The intervals are identified for you.

m3 = minor third   P4 = perfect fourth   P5 = perfect fifth   m6 = minor sixth   M6 = major sixth
m7 = minor seventh

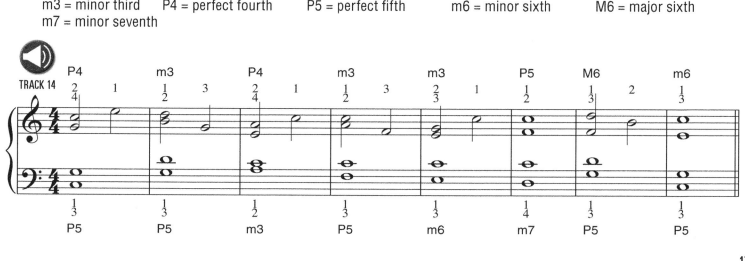

Identify the different interval leaps in the following two folksong arrangements.

CUTTING BRACKEN

Traditional Scottish

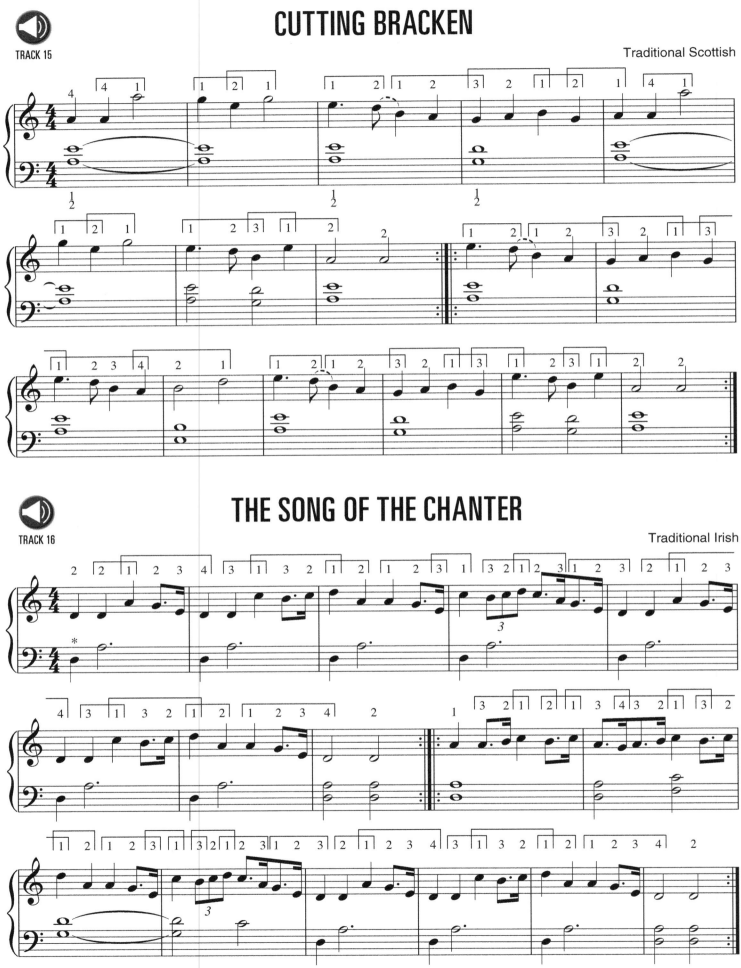

THE SONG OF THE CHANTER

Traditional Irish

* L.H. uses perfect fifths throughout.

KEY SIGNATURE RECAP AND SCALES

There are 15 key signatures and each major key has a relative minor scale, one that uses the same sharps and flats as its relative major. The relative minor scale begins a minor third (three half steps) below the tonic of the major scale. For example, the relative minor of C major is A minor, three half steps below.

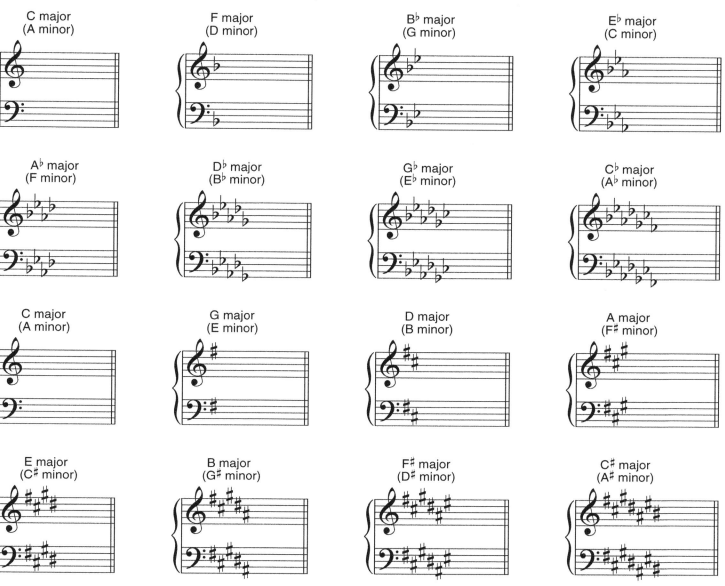

Scales are a great exercise for both familiarizing yourself with different key signatures and practicing good hand technique. Try these two octave scales in the following keys: C, G, D, A, and F major.

C MAJOR SCALE (TWO OCTAVES)

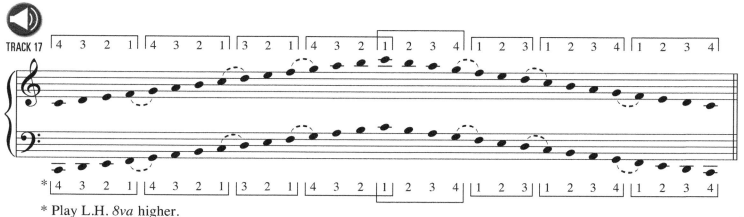

TRACK 17

* Play L.H. *8va* higher.

G MAJOR SCALE (TWO OCTAVES)

TRACK 18

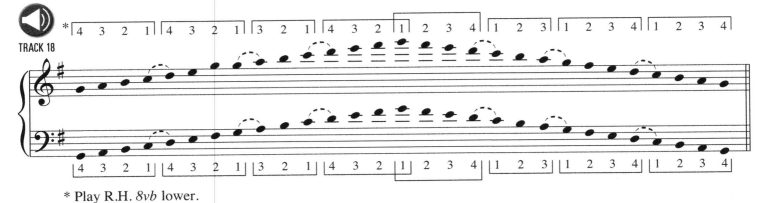

* Play R.H. *8vb* lower.

D MAJOR SCALE (TWO OCTAVES)

TRACK 19

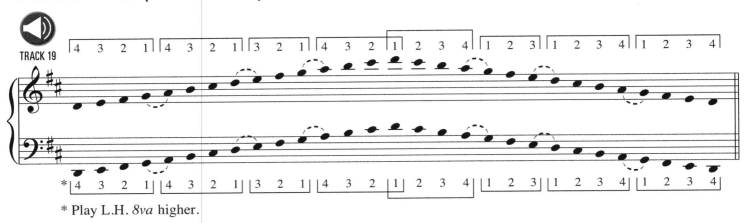

* Play L.H. *8va* higher.

A MAJOR SCALE (TWO OCTAVES)

TRACK 20

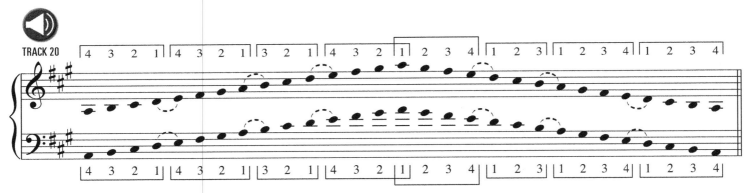

F MAJOR SCALE (TWO OCTAVES)

TRACK 21

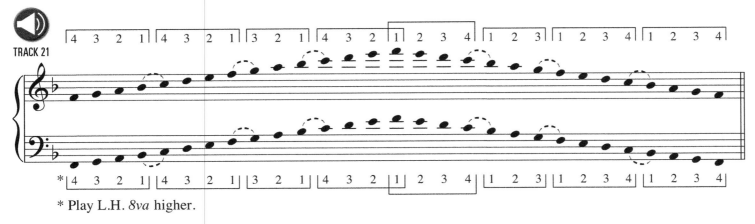

* Play L.H. *8va* higher.

TIME SIGNATURES

The **time signature** specifies how many beats are in each measure. The bottom number tells us the length of the beats themselves while the top number specifies how many of them are in each measure. For example: The time signature of 4/4 tells us that there are four (top number) quarter notes (bottom number) in each measure. The time signature of 6/8 tells us that there are six (top number) eighth notes (bottom number) in each measure. The time signature of 3/4 tells us that there are three (top number) quarter notes (bottom number) in each measure, and so on.

Here are three arrangements of tunes in 3/4 time, sometimes called "waltz time."

FEAR A BHÀTA

TRACK 22

Gaelic Folksong

DA DAY DAWN

Traditional Shetland Air

TRACK 23

Slowly, freely

TRACK 24

HECTOR THE HERO

Words by Thomas McWilliam
Music by James Scott Skinner

Note about phrasing vs. fingering: Depending on how one chooses to phrase a line, we may need to break some of our directional finger rules. Remember that the music always comes first!

ARPEGGIOS

An **arpeggio** is a musical technique where the notes of a chord are played one after another in sequence rather than being played at the same time. People often associate this "broken chord" with the harp and indeed the term itself comes from the Italian word "arpeggiare," which means "to play on a harp." The layout of the strings allows us to play arpeggios easily.

C MAJOR ARPEGGIO

TRACK 25

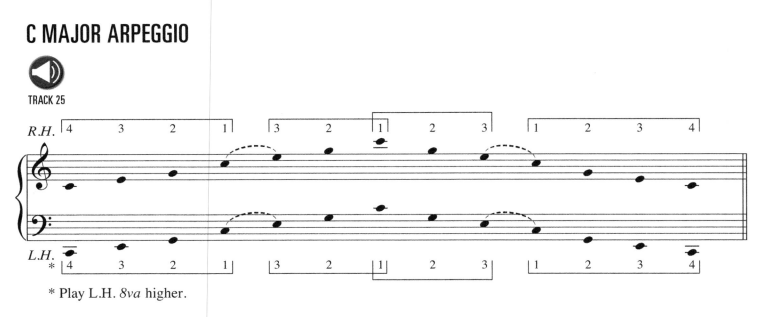

* Play L.H. *8va* higher.

Play the following arpeggios in both hands, using the same fingerings as the C major arpeggio.

G MAJOR ARPEGGIO

TRACK 26

D MAJOR ARPEGGIO

TRACK 27

A MAJOR ARPEGGIO

TRACK 28

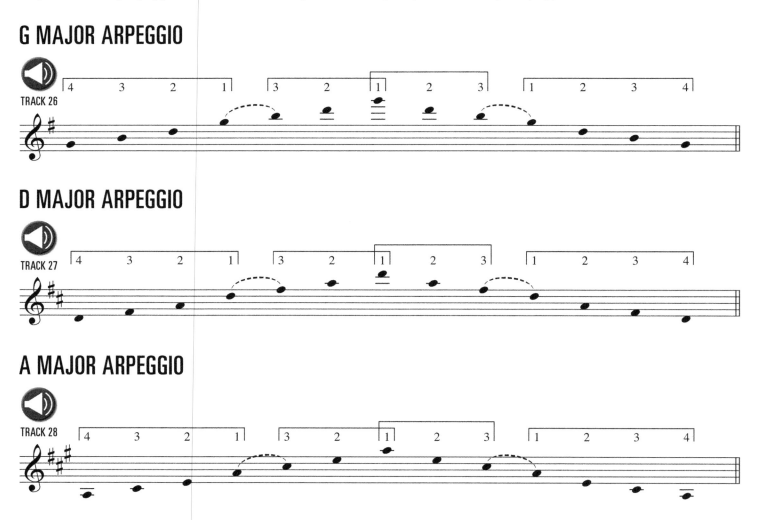

F MAJOR ARPEGGIO

TRACK 29

Try major arpeggios in your other available keys using the root, third, and fifth of the chord. If your harp has a limited range, try changing octaves and swapping hands. It is very important to keep stretching your hands into different positions and to become familiar with different intervals. This will increase your all-round dexterity.

Here are some four-note arpeggios that will challenge your fingers. Play these in both hands, as demonstrated on the audio tracks.

CMAJ7 ARPEGGIO

TRACK 30

ALTERNATIVE ARPEGGIO 1

TRACK 31

ALTERNATIVE ARPEGGIO 2

TRACK 32

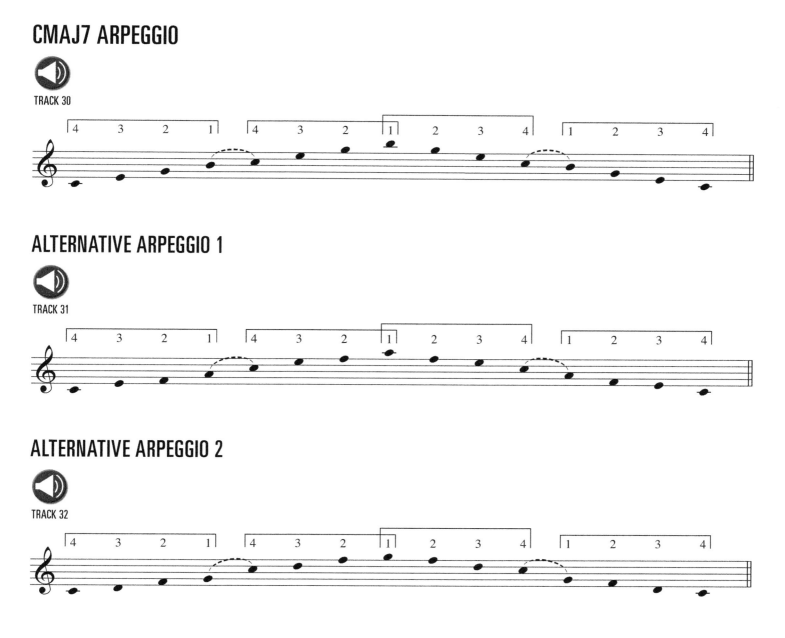

"Nora's Dove" and "A Minor Air" both use arpeggio accompaniment figures in the left hand.

NORA'S DOVE

American Folksong

TRACK 33

A MINOR AIR

TRACK 34

Traditional

I-IV-V CHORDS

The I-IV-V chords form the backbone of harmony. One might call them harmony's "primary colors." They are the chords based on the root (first note) of the scale, the subdominant (fourth note) of the scale, and the dominant (fifth note) of the scale. Between these three chords we have the harmonic foundation for thousands of songs and tunes.

By practicing the I-IV-V progression in different keys, you'll be opening many musical doors and will be able to enjoy jamming along with other musicians in a variety of musical settings.

In the following example, you see a C major scale with triads built upon the first, fourth, and fifth degress of the scale. This is how to locate the I, IV, and V chords.

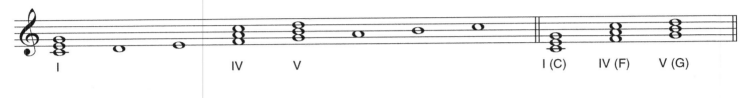

Other common keys include G major, D major, and F major. As with C major, levers will be involved.

G MAJOR

D MAJOR

F MAJOR

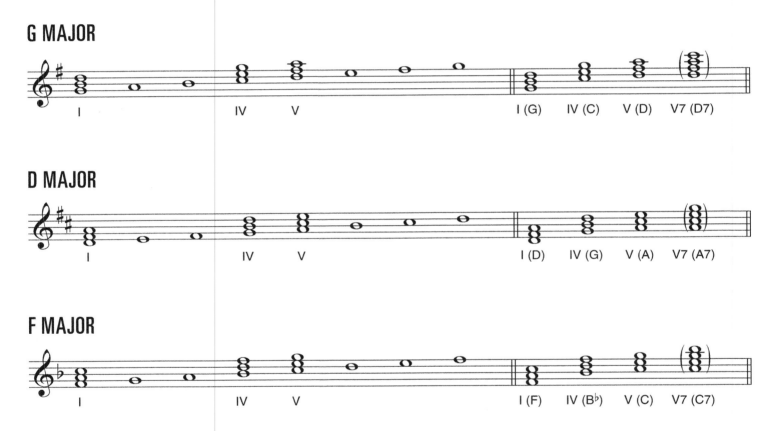

Now try for yourself, creating your own accompaniments for the following tunes and songs using the I-IV-V chords. First check that you are in the correct key and then enjoy working out your own arrangements. Try getting a friend to play the melody while you accompany them. This is when the real fun begins.

BEAUTIFUL BROWN EYES

TRACK 35

Traditional Folksong

Chorus

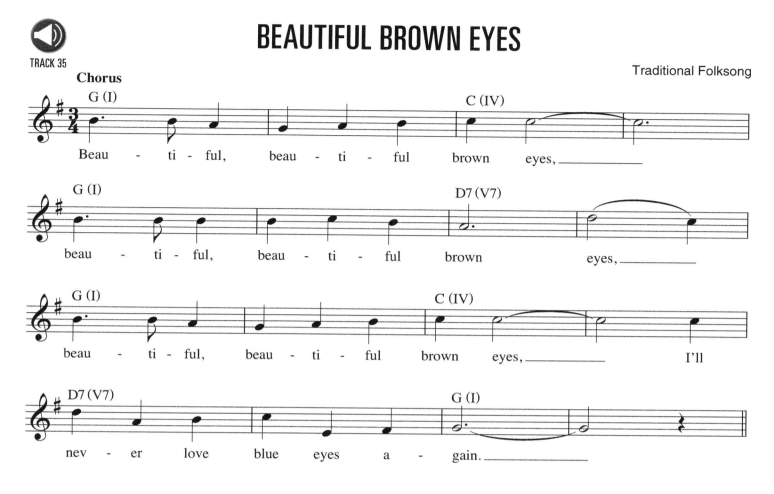

Additional Lyrics

1. Willie, I love you, my darling.
   I love you with all my heart.
   Tomorrow we might have been married,
   But ramblin' has kept us apart
   Chorus

2. Down through the barroom he staggered
   And fell down by the door.
   The very last words that he uttered,
   "I'll never see brown eyes no more."
   Chorus

AULD LANG SYNE
(ORIGINAL MELODY)

Words by Robert Burns
Traditional Scottish Melody

Chorus

Additional Lyrics

1. And surely ye'll be your pint-stowp!
   And surely I'll be mine!
   And we'll tak' a cup o' kindness yet
   For auld lang syne.
   Chorus

2. We twa hae run about the braes
   And pu'd the gowans fine;
   But we've wander'd mony a weary foot
   Sin auld lang syne.
   Chorus

3. We twa hae paidl'd i' the burn,
   Frae mornin' sun till dine;
   But seas between us braid hae roar'd
   Sin auld lang syne.
   Chorus

4. And there's a hand, my trusty fiere!
   And gie's a hand o' thine!
   And we'll tak' a right guid willy waught,
   For auld lang syne.
   Chorus

AE FOND KISS

Words by Robert Burns
Traditional Scottish Melody

TRACK 37

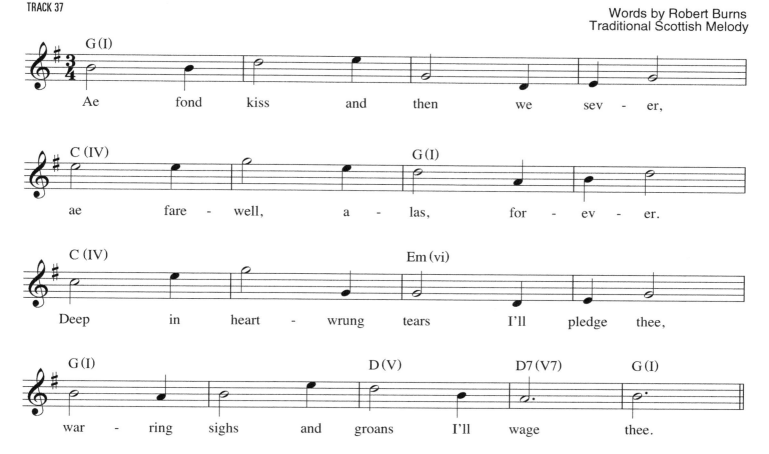

Ae fond kiss and then we sev - er,
ae fare - well, a - las, for - ev - er.
Deep in heart - wrung tears I'll pledge thee,
war - ring sighs and groans I'll wage thee.

Additional Lyrics

2. Who shall say that Fortune grieves him,
While the star of hope she leaves him?
Me nae cheerful twinkle lights me,
Dark despair around benights me.

3. I'll ne'er blame my partial fancy:
Nothing could resist my Nancy.
But to see her was to love her
Love but her, and love forever.

4. Had we never lo'ed sae kindly,
Had we never lo'ed sae blindly,
Never met – nor never parted –
We had ne'er been brokenhearted.

5. Fare thee weel, thou first and fairest,
Fare thee weel, thou best and dearest.
Thine be ilka joy and treasure,
Peace, enjoyment, love, and pleasure.

6. Ae fond kiss and then we sever,
Ae farewell, alas, forever.
Deep in heart-wrung tears I'll pledge thee,
Warring sighs and groans I'll wage thee.

FAIR AND TENDER LADIES

Kentucky Folksong

1. Come all ye fair _____ and ten - der la - dies, be care - ful how _____ you court young men. They're like a star _____ on a sum - mer's morn - ing: they'll first ap - pear _____ and then they're gone. _____ 2. They'll tell you ...wing. _____

Additional Lyrics

2. Do you remember our days of courting,
   When your head lay upon my breast?
   You could make me believe with falling of your arm
   That the sun rose in the West.

3. They'll tell you some loving story,
   They'll declare to you their love is true,
   Then they will go and court some other,
   And that's the love they have for you.

4. But no, I'm not a little sparrow,
   I have no wings with which to fly.
   So I sit here in grief and sorrow,
   To weep and pass my troubles by.

5. I wish I was a little sparrow
   And I had wings with which to fly
   Right over to see my false true-lover,
   To give him a slap for ev'ry lie.

6. If I had known, before I courted,
   That love was such a killing thing,
   I'd a-locked my heart in a chest of iron,
   And tied it down so it couldn't take wing.

TRACK 39

ERISKAY LOVE LILT

Hebrides Folksong

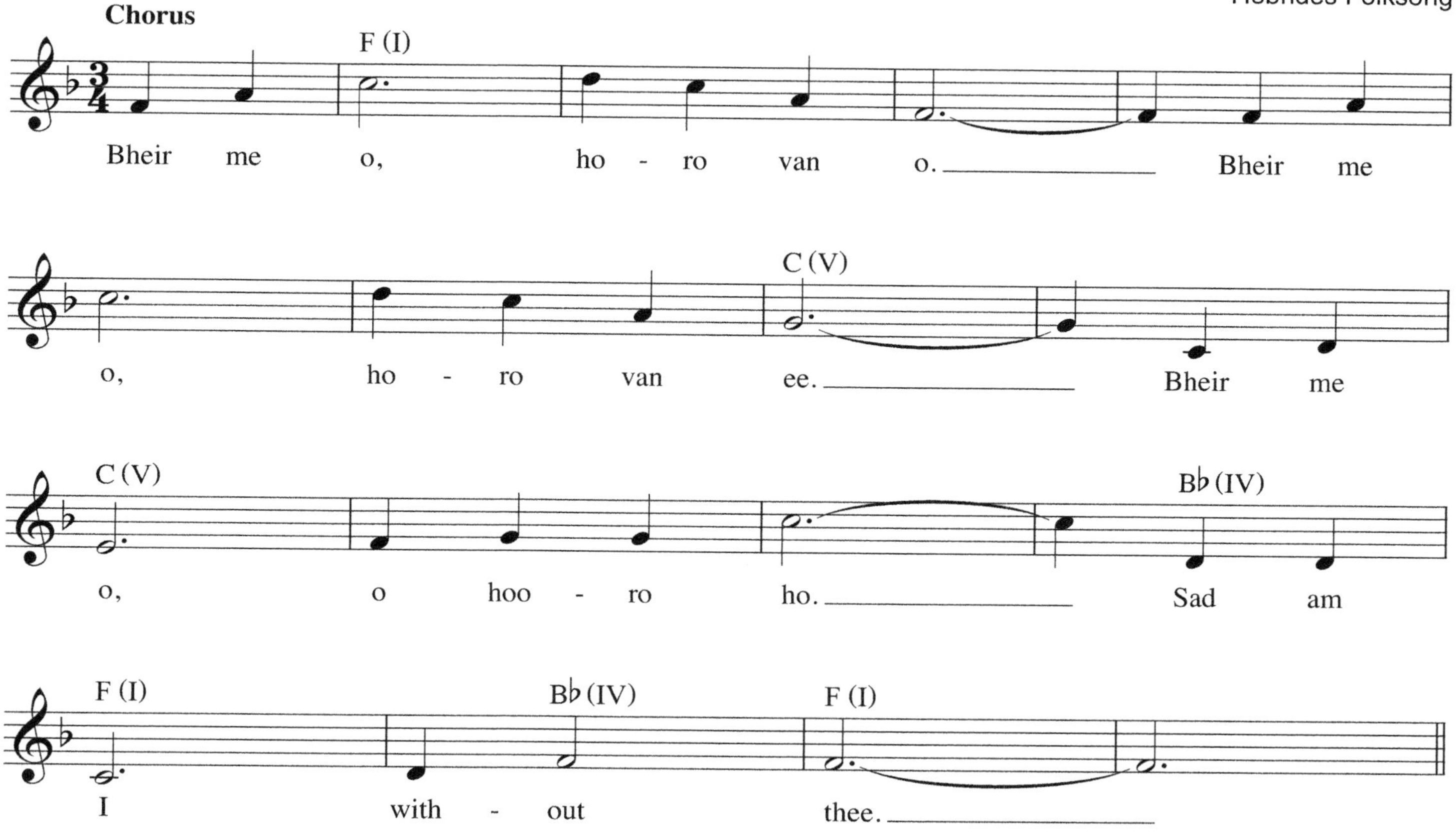

Chorus
F (I)
Bheir me o, ho - ro van o.
Bheir me o, ho - ro van
C (V)
ee.
Bheir me
C (V)
o, o hoo - ro ho.
B♭ (IV)
Sad am
F (I)
I
B♭ (IV)
with - out
F (I)
thee.

Additional Lyrics

1. When I'm lonely, dear white heart,
   Black the night and wild the sea,
   By love's light my foot finds
   The old pathway to thee.
   Chorus

2. Thou'rt the music of my heart,
   Harp of joy, o cuit mo chridh,
   Moon of guidance by night,
   Strength and light thou'rt to me.
   Chorus

3. In the morning, when I go
   To the white and shining sea,
   In the calling of the seals
   Thy soft calling to me.
   Chorus

MY BONNIE LIES OVER THE OCEAN

Scottish Folksong

TRACK 40

Additional Lyrics

O blow ye winds over the ocean,
O blow ye winds over the sea.
O blow ye winds over the ocean,
And bring back my Bonnie to me.
Chorus

Last night as I lay on my pillow,
Last night as I lay on my bed,
Last night as I lay on my pillow,
I dreamed that my Bonnie was dead.
Chorus

The winds have blown over the ocean,
The winds have blown over the sea,
The winds have blown over the ocean,
And brought back my Bonnie to me.
Chorus

34

YE BANKS AND BRAES

Words by Robert Burns
Old Scottish Melody

Additional Lyrics

Aft hae I rov'd by bonnie Doon,
To see the rose and woodbine twine.
And ilka bird sang o' its love,
And fondly sae did I o' mine.
Wi' lightsome heart I pu'd a rose,
Fu' sweet upon its thorny tree.
But my fause lover stole my rose,
And ah! he left the thorn wi' me.

OSTINATOS

An **ostinato** is a recurring pattern or motif. Ostinato-based exercises are a great way to tackle three elements of harp playing:

- **Hand independence.** One of the unique things about playing the harp is the fact that we have two hands, two separate voices. The more we focus on strengthening each hand as an independent voice, the more we shall be able to utilize our instrument fully and to come up with interesting arrangements and compositions.

- **Hand technique.** As we move through these ostinato exercises, be sure to check on your hand technique constantly, bringing your fingers into a fist and pushing your thumb up on the strings.

- **Rhythm.** Rhythm is what breathes life into the notes. I'd recommend working with a metronome, particularly if you're used to playing solo. By focusing on rhythm we will improve our accuracy of attack and confidence of sound. It will also make it much easier to work with other musicians when the time comes.

LEFT-HAND OSTINATO

Here is an example of an ostinato. Make sure the ostinato itself is solid and steady before bringing in the right-hand patterns.

Now gradually begin introducing the right-hand patterns given in the exercises below.

EXERCISE 1 (HALF NOTES)

TRACK 42

EXERCISE 2 (HALF NOTES STARTING ON BEAT 2)

TRACK 43

EXERCISE 3 (QUARTER NOTES)

TRACK 44

EXERCISE 4 (EIGHTH NOTES)

TRACK 45

Now alternate the right-hand patterns while keeping the left hand steady.

RIGHT-HAND OSTINATO

Let's switch hands. It feels quite different, but it is important to try and strengthen the hands in equal measure. Here, the right hand takes the ostinato.

In the eighth-note example on page 38 (Exercise 4), be sure to keep the left-hand wrist very loose. Your elbow should float out to support your wrist and hand.

EXERCISE 1 (HALF NOTES)

EXERCISE 2 (HALF NOTES)

EXERCISE 3 (QUARTER NOTES)

EXERCISE 4 (EIGHTH NOTES)

Make up your own ostinatos. They can be based on anything and are a constant challenge and excellent exercise. Here are some ideas to get you started. Stabilize these in your left hand before starting to bring in different patterns in the right hand.

Left-Hand Ostinato Examples

Here are two arrangements that use ostinato-based accompaniments, "The Christ Child's Lullaby" and "I Remember Purple." Make your left hand musical, phrasing and treating it as a countermelody.

THE CHRIST CHILD'S LULLABY

TRACK 46

Hebrides Folksong

I REMEMBER PURPLE

Traditional

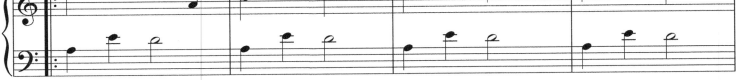

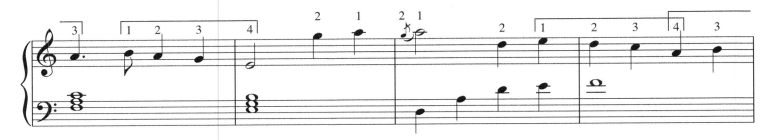

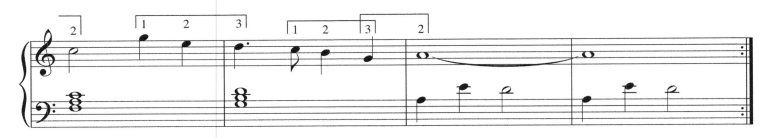

TRIPLETS

The Celtic repertoire seems tailor-made for the folk harp. It is a prominent instrument in the traditional music of Scotland and Ireland. The **triplet** is a technique that is commonly used in tunes from both these countries. It should be played with great clarity. While the following exercises aim to demonstrate the triplet in a practical sense, its "feel" can really be learned only from listening to traditional Irish and Scottish music.

The triplet is a series of three repeated pitches that usually fill the space of a quarter note. They can be purely decorative or they can be used to keep the rhythm flowing. On the harp, there are various ways of fingering these triplets, the most common being 4-3-2, though 3-2-3 or 2-3-2 are also valid fingerings. When playing triplets, I like to anchor my thumb on an upper string whenever possible, grounding my hand as I play these rapidly repeating notes.

Start by playing your triplets slowly, gradually speeding up while maintaining clarity. Try leaning on each finger to make sure all are strengthened equally before switching to a perfectly even sound.

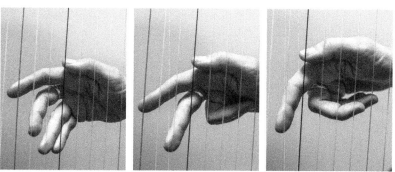

The 4th finger plays the string first, followed immediately by the 3rd finger and then the 2nd finger, almost as if it were all one circular movement.

EXERCISE 1

TRACK 48
(slow)

TRACK 49
(fast)

Anchor the thumb on C and play the exercise above slowly, making sure that all the repeated notes are clear and even. Speed up gradually

EXERCISE 2

TRIPLET ETUDE

TRACK 50

THE SLIDE

The **slide** is a fingering technique used in traditional Irish and Scottish harp playing. It is used to finger two adjacent notes by sliding the thumb between the two. This is a fast and efficient way to finger up-tempo tunes and to create a *legato* sound.

NOTE: While slides are a great fingering choice for smoothing out "note-y" passages, there is always the option of an alternative fingering. Play around with different fingering ideas and make a choice that's right for you.

There follow several traditional Celtic tunes that incorporate triplets and slides in the melodies

THE ROLLING WAVE

TRACK 51

Traditional Irish

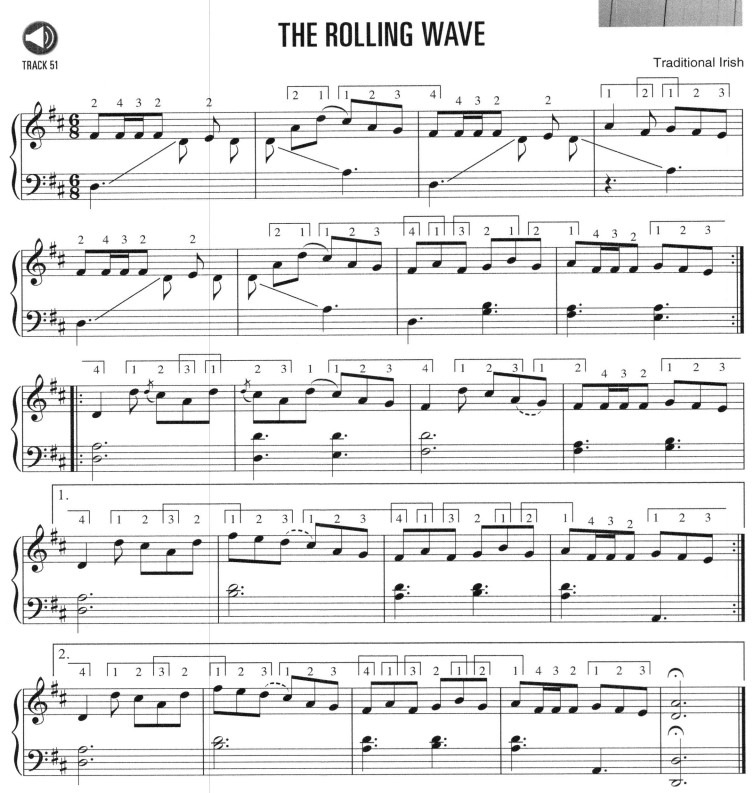

THE KILFENORA JIG

Traditional Irish

THE FAIRY DANCE

Traditional

WILLAFJORD

Traditional Shetland

TRACK 54

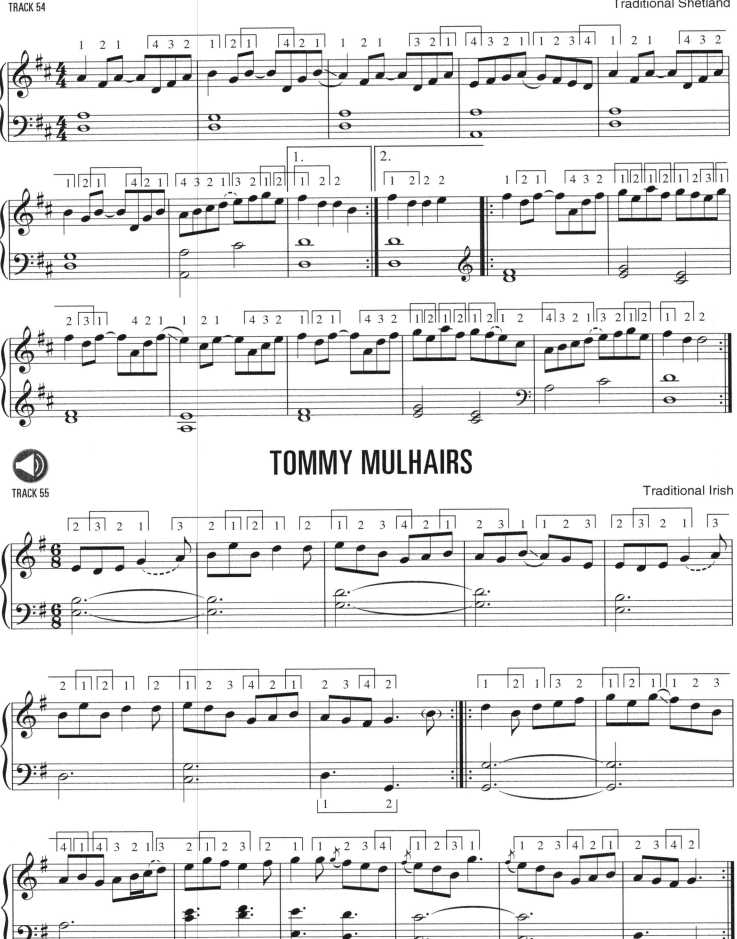

TOMMY MULHAIRS

Traditional Irish

TRACK 55

44

ELEANOR PLUNKETT

By Turlough O'Carolan

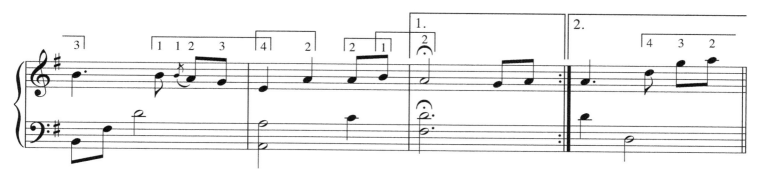

Turlough O'Carolan (1670–1738) was a blind Irish harpist, singer, and composer whose great fame is due to his gift for writing beautiful melodies. Many consider him to be Ireland's national composer. Quite a few of his tunes have become standards of the Irish harping repertoire.

NOTE: For the songs on pages 42–45, any written ornamentation is to be added after the melody is learned. For the most part, I have left ornaments unfingered. These are stylistic suggestions and should not take away from the clarity of the melody. As you become more familiar with the tunes, play around with your own ornamentation ideas.

AUDIO TRACK LISTING

1. Two-finger exercise
2. Two-finger etude
3. Triads (descending)
4. Triads (ascending)
5. Triads (alternative)
6. Four-finger exercise (ascending)
7. Four-finger exercise (descending)
8. Four-finger exercise (alternative)
9. Frère Jacques
10. Hymn
11. Katie Bairdie
12. A Minor Tune
13. Breton Tune
14. Interval exercise
15. Cutting Bracken
16. The Song of the Chanter
17. C major scale (two octaves)
18. G major scale (two octaves)
19. D major scale (two octaves)

20. A major scale (two octaves)
21. F major scale
22. Fear a Bhàta
23. Da Day Dawn
24. Hector the Hero
25. C major arpeggio
26. G major arpeggio
27. D major arpeggio
28. A major arpeggio
29. F major arpeggio
30. Cmaj7 arpeggio
31. Alternative Arpeggio 1
32. Alternative Arpeggio 2
33. Nora's Dove
34. A Minor Air
35. Beautiful Brown Eyes
36. Auld Lang Syne
37. Ae Fond Kiss
38. Fair and Tender Ladies

39. Eriskay Love Lilt
40. My Bonnie Lies Over the Ocean
41. Ye Banks and Braes
42. Ostinato exercise 1
43. Ostinato exercise 2
44. Ostinato exercise 3
45. Ostinato exercise 4
46. The Christ Child's Lullaby
47. I Remember Purple
48. Triplet exercise 1 (slow)
49. Triplet execise 1 (fast)
50. Triplet etude
51. The Rolling Wave
52. The Kilfenora Jig
53. The Fairy Dance
54. Willafjord
55. Tommy Mulhairs
56. Eleanor Plunkett

ABOUT THE AUTHOR

Harpist, singer, and educator **Maeve Gilchrist** was born in Edinburgh, Scotland. Immersed in traditional Scottish music from a young age, Maeve studied at the City of Edinburgh Music School and later as a full scholarship recipient from the Berklee College of Music, Boston. She has been credited as an innovator of the Clarsach (Scottish Harp) due to her uniquely chromatic style of playing and improvising. Maeve is currently based in New York City, touring internationally on a regular basis and teaching harp at the Berklee College of Music. Performance highlights include the Tanglewood Jazz Festival, Delfest, the World Harp Congress, the International German Harp Tour, the Boston Pops Jazz Festival, and the Celtic Connections Festival. She has released two self-titled albums on the Adventure Music label as well as a self-released solo harp venture called *The Ostinato Project*, a series of compositions focused on utilizing both hands as separate voices.

ACKNOWLEDGMENTS

I wish to extend my heartfelt thanks to the following: the Berklee College of Music, the City of Edinburgh Music School, and all my wonderful teachers over the years; Dusty Strings, Thormahlen Harps, and Frank Sievert; Matt Smith, Club Passim, and all of the Boston Music Scene; Jim and Anne Gilchrist; Mairead and Conor Doherty; Stephen Webber and Aaron Silverstein.